My Very First
First-Aid
Book

*A Simple Guide to First Aid
for Younger Children*

My Very First First-Aid Book

A Simple Guide to First Aid for Younger Children

Ian Lees

ATHENA PRESS
LONDON

My Very First First-Aid Book
A Simple Guide to First Aid for Younger Children
Copyright © Ian Lees 2009
Illustrated by Neil Gange

All Rights Reserved

ISBN 978 1 84748 649 3

First published 2009 by
ATHENA PRESS
Queen's House, 2 Holly Road
Twickenham TW1 4EG
United Kingdom

Printed for Athena Press

Especially for Freya, Harvey, Lauren and Sophie

Contents

Introduction

My very first FIRST-AID book
Will help me to help others.
It might be my mum or my dad,
Or my friends, or sisters or brothers.

So, this book is written to help you
To learn about basic FIRST AID.
You can learn a little each day,
Just in case your memory should fade.

Simple things that happen at school
And at home often cause alarm.
Wouldn't it be cool if you knew FIRST AID
To stop any further harm?

Calling for help

If you come across an accident,
You have to get help right away –
Dial 999 immediately*
Without any fuss or delay.

A person will ask you quite calmly,
'Which service do you require?'
Ask for the one you have chosen –
Ambulance, Police or Fire.

First give the accident location,
Then give your name and address.
Say exactly what's happened
And the operator will do the rest.

---

* Only applicable in the United Kingdom. Outside the UK please dial your
selected emergency telephone number.

Order of priorities

Remember:
Breathing and bleeding,
Fractures and burns;
A check in this order
Does the patient good turns.

Bites from pets

Pets can make the best of friends
If you should treat them right.
But if you make them angry
They will sometimes turn and bite.

So, if a pet decides to bite
And puncture marks are made,
Washing the wound in warm water
Shows that you know your first aid.

When washing, encourage the wound to bleed –
This helps flush the germs away –
Then go to a doctor just to make sure
That your first aid has saved the day.

Bruises

Bruises can sometimes be painful
To treat them, here's what to do:
Put on some cold water padding
To help them stop turning blue.

Scratches and cuts

Sometimes, when we're playing about,
We might get a nasty scratch or cut.
Wash in warm water to get the dirt out
And if needed, a plaster should be put.

Burns

Burns can be very painful;
Treatment must be quick.
Soak with lots of cold water –
The blisters DO NOT prick.

Remove items like bangles and rings
Then wrap in a towel clean and dry.
DO NOT put on any cream
But go straight to a hospital nearby.

Care with matches

Please DON'T play with matches –
That's a lesson to be learnt.
Children who ignore this rule
Are often badly burnt.

Fainting

Poor Harvey had fainted at school;
He felt giddy and fell to the ground.
It's lucky that Freya remembered the rule
And quickly she brought him around.

She kept him lying down on the floor
With his feet off the ground just a bit.
She loosened all his tight clothing
And he soon came round feeling fit.

Foreign bodies – in the eye

Lauren had something stuck in her eye,
When she blinked it hurt quite a bit.
She sensibly went to her teacher,
Who took out a small piece of grit.

Foreign bodies – in the nose or ear

So, if something is stuck in your nose or ear,
Then please DON'T poke about.
Go straight away to an adult
And ask them to please take it out.

Foreign bodies – in the throat

A fish bone stuck in your throat
Often causes alarm,
Go to hospital if you can't remove it
Or it may cause further harm.

Nosebleeds

Here's what to do for a nosebleed:
Get as near as you can to fresh air,
Breathe through your mouth and lean forward,
Preferably sat on a chair.

Remember to loosen tight collars,
Pinch the nose between finger and thumb.
Make sure that you keep nice and warm
And your job as First Aider is done.

People feeling very, very cold

Infants and old folk, who are extremely cold,
You'll find their skin very cold to touch.
Their pulse will be slow,
Their breathing low
And they won't like it very much.

So wrap them in really warm blankets,
Give them something to drink, warm and sweet.
If they're not to fade,
Then get medical aid,
But remember, don't use extreme heat.

The danger of smoking

Smoking is not very healthy
And it makes your breath smell too.
Your lungs should be pink,
So please stop and think
Or the next victim could be you.

Sophie thought she was clever
In smoking her first cigarette.
It wasn't a joke
When she choked on the smoke –
She hasn't recovered just yet.

Playing near water

Jeremy loved his big brother;
They went down to the river to play.
They found an old tank,
Lying there on the bank
And together they floated away.

The tank had a hole in the bottom;
The river was fast and deep.
Neither could swim –
What a mess they were in –
And Jeremy started to weep.

A fisherman happened to see them,
He knew of the danger ahead.
He saw the boys' fear,
As they rushed to the weir
And to their assistance he sped.

Please think when you go out to play.
Don't do things silly or daft.
If you play in the wet,
It's a safe enough bet,
To be supervised in some proper craft.

Poisonous berries

Becky once saw some strange berries,
Which looked very nice to chew.
So she ate three or four
Then couldn't eat more,
As she felt really ill
And turned blue.

So remember that eating strange berries
Is a thing which shouldn't be done.
It's important to empty the tummy
And Becky didn't find that much fun.

It's important to get to a doctor,
Or hospital if it is near.
Just to make sure that the tummy
Is empty and perfectly clear.

Shock

The patient feels cold all over,
And their face is ever so pale.
Sweat may be seen on their forehead
And unconsciousness may soon prevail.

Try to keep the patient warm and still;
Raise the feet a little off ground.
Work quickly and loosen tight clothing;
Avoid any loud sudden sounds.

Breathing is quicker than normal
And a crowd might well be there.
Tell them to stand well back
To give the patient fresh air.

Make sure the patient can breathe;
Make sure no further dangers are near.
Then call for an ambulance at once,
Making sure the area's kept clear.

Splinters

Splinters are not very healthy
And sometimes they hurt quite a lot.
Clean tweezers and some antiseptic,
Will help you more often than not.

Sometimes you can take them out yourself,
But keep the area nice and clean.
Just gently ease out the splinter
Making sure nothing's left where it's been.

Sprains

Robert played football at school.
He played one day in the rain;
He twisted his ankle on scoring
And the teacher diagnosed a sprain.

The ankle swelled up all at once;
There was loss of power and much pain.
Robert felt awfully sick
As he lay in the pouring rain.

Luckily the teacher knew what to do
And strapped his ankle up tight,
By using some padding and a bandage –
He knew his first aid all right.

If in doubt then treat as a fracture,
Take to hospital straight away.
For in order to confirm the damage,
The patient should have an X-ray.

Stings

Bee stings and wasp stings are not very nice.
Though the wasp does take his sting out,
The bee, he leaves his sting behind,
And then flies off without.

The bee sting then should be removed
And special cream applied.
Wasp stings can with vinegar be dabbed,
From most houses this can be supplied.

Suffocation

Placing a plastic bag over the head
Is a dangerous thing to do.
You must promise never to do it
Or the next victim could be you.

Angela tried it once as a bet,
You see, she was easily led.
She found breathing hard and was giddy,
And her face was flushed quite red.

You have to make sure that the patient
Is lying on their side on the ground.
Make sure the airway is clear
And fresh air should bring them round.

Stroke victims

Shape of the face looks strange to you,
Talking is sometimes difficult too,
Raising of arms is impossible to do,
OK, now the rest is up to you –
Keeping calm, save valuable time,
Explain when you phone the ambulance line.

How to make your very own first-aid box

Now that you know how to do some really simple first aid, why not make up your very own first-aid box?

Ask your parents if they can let you have a shoe box in good condition, or maybe something a little stronger like a plastic ice cream tub complete with its lid.

These are most of the items which you will need to put in your first aid box.

- ✓ Some assorted waterproof plasters
- ✓ A selection of bandages
- ✓ A selection of sterile dressings, small, medium and large
- ✓ Some safety pins
- ✓ A pair of blunt-ended scissors
- ✓ A clean pair of tweezers
- ✓ Some triangular bandages
- ✓ 1 or 2 eye patches
- ✓ 2 or 3 pairs of latex disposable gloves
- ✓ A small bottle of disinfectant/antiseptic fluid.

It's also a good idea to make a list of the items you have in your box. Make sure that if you use any of the disposable items, you replace them as soon as possible.

Important

If you really enjoy helping people by having even a basic knowledge of first aid, and you want to learn more, why not contact one of the organisations which teach first aid to a higher standard. The British Red Cross or St Johns Ambulance services are only applicable to the UK. First-aid training organisations may be found in your local telephone directory.

Glossary
Some words in the book you might like help on

Antiseptic/Disinfectant	cream or liquid which kills germs
Diagnosed	identified, recognised
Encourage	hasten or urge, make happen
Foreign body	something which shouldn't be there
Fractures Bones	bones which have been broken
Germ	very small, microscopic cell, which causes disease
Location	the place where you are
Operator	the person who answers your 999 call
Sprain	pulling or tearing of a muscle
Supervised	looked after by an adult
Unconsciousness	asleep, does not respond to anything.

Made in the USA
Lexington, KY
12 June 2016